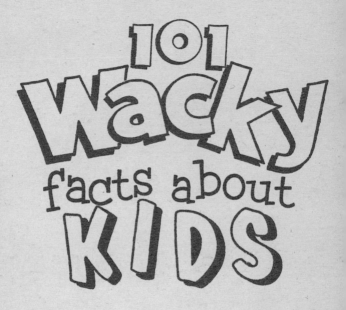

101 Wacky facts about KIDS

101 Wacky facts about KIDS

by C. E. Thompson

SCHOLASTIC INC.
New York Toronto London Auckland Sydney

ISBN 0-590-44890-0
Copyright © 1992 by Parachute Press Inc.
All rights reserved. Published by Scholastic Inc.

Designed by Paula Jo Smith
Illustrated by Bryan Hendrix

12 11 10 9 8 7 6 5 4   2 3 4 5 6/9

Printed in the U. S. A.   01

First Scholastic printing, January 1992

Chapter 1

WACKY FACTS
ABOUT KIDS

There are about 1 1/2 billion kids in the world! If they all lined up, the line would be about 1 million miles long. That's long enough to wrap around the Earth forty times!

What have children all over the world played for the past 4,000 years? Tug-of-war, that's what! This famed game is still a favorite of Egyptian, Eskimo, African, Chinese, and American kids.

The game of marbles is almost 1,000 years old! Marbles have been found in American Indian tombs and in ancient Egyptian pharaohs' tombs! In Turkey and Iran, kids play with marbles made from the knucklebones of sheep!

Blow out all your noodles! In China, kids eat bowls of long noodles on their birthday so they'll live long lives!

Do you want to join a circus? It's easy, at least in India. Around the age of three, some village girls with the consent of their parents, join the circus to be trained as acrobats!

Kids in Sweden don't have to worry about getting a spanking from their parents. Why? Spankings are against the law in that Scandinavian country!

Do you want to ride a crocodile? Then just go to West Africa! Crocodiles are sacred animals in Paga, a small village in Ghana. The villagers treat crocodiles with respect. They feed them live chickens and let their children play a game called "Riding the Crocodile"!

Baby love! When a certain couple was married in the Asian country of Bangladesh in 1986, the groom was eleven months old and the bride was just three months old! The families of the babies had been enemies for twenty years. They set up the match to help end their feud.

Pedal power! Unicycle riding is part of the curriculum at a school in Newbury, Ohio! Gym teachers require all the kids to ride! They encourage the students to practice as much as possible—even in the hallways between classes!

A twelve-year-old girl in England had a sneezing fit that lasted for two and a half years! Donna Griffiths sneezed about 1 million times in the first year—that's an average of two sneezes every minute! Luckily for her, she outgrew the sneezing fit!

Some birthday party! In Thailand, birthday kids don't receive gifts; instead they <u>give</u> them!

Oh, what beautiful eyes you have! In 1979 a boy in Cape Town, South Africa, had a seed and a sprout growing out of his left eye! Scientists who examined the seedling discovered that the sprout was soon to become a marigold. The seedling was surgically removed, and the boy's eye returned to normal!

Chapter Two

YOUR NOT-SO-WACKY BODY!

Healthy kids! People are usually the healthiest between the ages of five and fifteen years old.

Babies are <u>not</u> born with a belly button or navel. Babies inside the mother get their food and oxygen through a special cord that connects their belly to their mother. Upon birth, this cord is cut. The place on the belly where the cord used to be heals up and leaves a scar—the belly button!

Not a bad catch for a kid! A twelve-year-old boy discovered the fossil of a huge prehistoric fish near his home in Texas. The fish lived 100 million years ago and probably weighed about 600 pounds when it died!

You can smell about 10,000 different odors! "Smell cells" inside your nostrils have millions of little feelers that pick up different scents.

The nose knows! Kids have a better sense of smell than their grandparents! As the body ages, the sense of smell deteriorates more quickly than the other senses.

Most of your body is made of water! If a kid weighs 85 pounds, for example, he's carrying around more than 50 pounds of water in his cells!

Kids can't tickle themselves silly! That's what a team of scientists proved when they did an experiment with a boy's bare foot and a "tickling stick." The boy thought it hardly tickled at all when he used the stick to tickle his own bare foot. But when one of the researchers tickled the boy's foot, he could barely stand it.

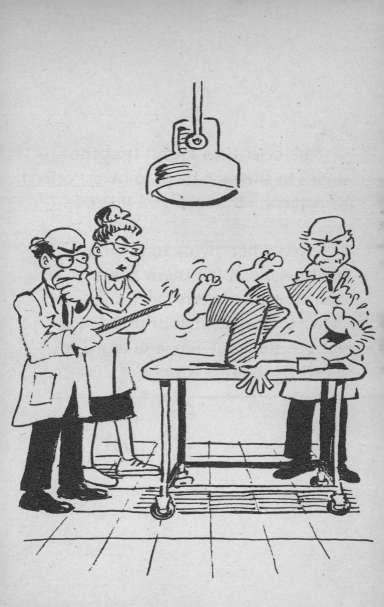

The scientists found that the nerves in the skin have to be <u>surprised</u> for someone to really feel tickled.

Even when twins look alike, most dogs can tell them apart! That's because every person has his or her own special odor and a dog can use its great sense of smell to tell which twin is which!

Twins may look exactly alike, but there's always one sure way to tell them apart—fingerprint them! Everybody has unique fingerprints, even twins.

A kid's brain weighs about 3 pounds—nearly as much as an adult's brain weighs! The brain and head double in size before a kid is two years old. But after he or she is six, the brain and head will hardly grow at all.

A kid's hair grows faster than an adult's! Hair can grow more than 6 inches a year, and grows fastest in the summer!

If you live in Florida, your nails grow faster than they would if you lived in Alaska! Why? Because nails grow faster in warm weather! Nails grow about .04 inch (1 mm) in ten days.

Growing pains! Kids can grow a foot taller between the ages of seven and twelve! Boys usually have a growth spurt when they're in their teens, but most kids grow fastest before they're two years old.

Just a wink! Your eyes blink at least six times a minute, sometimes more! The surface of the eye needs to stay moist, so it's hard for anyone to keep his or her eyes open for a whole minute—unless they're underwater!

Shivering in the cold keeps you warmer! Your muscles contract when you shiver, which makes the muscle cells burn more fuel. So your body can create heat to warm you even when you're standing still!

What makes you itch? A little pain, that's what! Mosquito bites, poison ivy, and allergies irritate pain nerves in the skin and cause the itch!

For most of his life, David Phillip lived inside of a giant plastic bubble! His body had no immune system to fight disease, so he always had to stay within the germ-free environment of his bubble. When David was six years old, NASA gave him a space suit, which allowed him to walk around his house and even go outside for the first time.

Chapter Three

I'M A WACKY DOODLE DANDY

Oh no! It <u>is</u> legal in the United States for parents to tell their kids when to go to bed!

Mayflower babies! About thirty children came to America aboard the Mayflower and were part of the Plymouth colony. Two babies were born during the ocean voyage!

During the Revolutionary War, a sixteen-year-old girl rode her horse all night through the Connecticut countryside, warning the colonials of the British attack! Sybil Ludington was the daughter of a colonel in the militia. She rode 40 miles—farther than Paul Revere rode!

She changed the face of history! An eleven-year-old, Grace Bedell, talked Abraham Lincoln into growing a beard. She wrote a letter telling Lincoln she thought a beard would make his thin face look nicer. He became the first U.S. president to wear a beard!

Do you want a drink? Babies born to pioneer settlers were sometimes given a wine bath! This was supposed to make the baby strong (or strong smelling?).

Mail or fe-mail? In 1914 a four-year-old girl was sent through the mail from one town in Idaho to another! Her parents couldn't afford the railroad ticket to send their daughter to relatives for a visit, so they mailed her instead! Live chicks were shipped through the mail in those days, so the little girl was labeled as a baby chick.

Hey, Mom! Hey, Dad! Let's move down south! Why? Because there's no law that kids have to go to school in Mississippi!

Forward march! Imagine a ten-year-old boy going to war! During the Civil War, some drummer boys were that young. "Johnny Shiloh" was the nickname of a drummer boy who became a popular hero after his drum had been hit by an artillery shell. He survived!

Don't tickle me or I'll have you arrested! One of the wackiest laws ever passed in Norton, Virginia, made tickling a girl illegal!

Mark Twain's hometown of Hannibal, Missouri, celebrates Tom Sawyer Day with a fence-painting race! Kids dress up like Tom Sawyer and whitewash a fence, as Tom was supposed to do in the book by Mark Twain.

Chapter Four

YOUNG AND FAMOUS

The king's curse! When he was only five years old, Louis the Fourteenth of France was crowned king. Nevertheless, his mother made the king stay in his room for two days after he said a swear word!

When Henry Chambers's mother told him to "go out and play" she didn't mean in the garden! In 1913 Henry was only eleven years old when he became the organist at a cathedral in England.

Read all about it! Thomas Edison published his own newspaper when he was twelve years old! It cost three cents, and he sold it to passengers on the railroad where he worked selling candy and city newspapers.

Picky picky! Even as a boy, the famous escape artist Harry Houdini was especially good at picking locks. He regularly broke into the locked cupboard where his mom kept the cake and cookies.

Million-dollar baby! Child movie star Jackie Coogan was the first kid to earn a million dollars! He was six years old in 1920 when he costarred with Charlie Chaplin in the famous film classic <u>The Kid</u>.

Chapter Five

THOSE WERE THE DAYS!

OWo....

It's against the law in Elkhart, Indiana, for a barber to tell a squirming child, "Sit still or I'll cut off your ears!"

Kid crusaders! Thousands of children tried to march from France and Germany to Jerusalem during the Children's Crusade of 1212! Many boys and girls on the march were under twelve years old!

Ribbit! In the 1500s European children with whooping cough had to undergo an interesting "treatment"—holding live frogs in their mouths!

In the 1600s English boys under seven years old wore skirts instead of pants! Boys in ancient Egypt and in Scotland also wore skirts. In Scotland, boys (and men) still wear skirts on occasion. The skirts are called kilts.

In 1843 a little boy in India was carried off by a she-wolf while his mother worked in the fields. He was found a few years later running with a pack of wolf cubs and identified by a scar he had on his knee! The wolf-child never adapted to human ways. In 1851 he escaped into the jungles and was never seen again!

Off with their heads! A seven-year-old boy became the official executioner of France in 1726! The job of executioner was passed down from father to son, and when his father died, young Jean-Baptiste Sanson inherited the job. Although he was too small to actually perform the beheadings, Jean-Baptiste supervised the executions until he was eighteen years old. Then <u>he</u> took over the beheadings himself!

Alice in Wonderland actually lived! Her full name was Alice Liddell. She and her sisters often listened to stories told to them by Charles Dodgson, better known as Lewis Carroll. In fact it was on an outing with Alice and her sisters that he created the story of a little girl who falls asleep and dreams she goes down a rabbit hole! The real Alice grew up to be an intelligent and beautiful woman.

In the twenties and thirties candy bars cost only a nickel and a movie cost ten or fifteen cents. Kids in those days made about fifteen cents an hour for baby-sitting and twenty-five cents for mowing a lawn!

Kids in Missouri once built an entire town! In 1925, for a school project, kids made a toy town on 6 acres of land in a city park. The town had 400 little buildings that looked exactly like normal-sized ones!

Shirley Temple, the child movie star of the thirties and forties, made a million dollars by the age of ten!

In 1929 kids in Baltimore started a new craze—flagpole-sitting! Twelve-year-old Jimmy Jones sat on the platform of a 25-foot flagpole for 250 hours—more than ten days!

Lurline! Myrna! Patience! Hazel! If you were born fifty years ago you probably would have been given one of these names! Luckily for you, popular names today are Jessica, Melissa, Jennifer, Samantha, Stephanie, and Tiffany!

Shirley, are you a boy or a girl? In the 19th century Shirley was a popular name for a boy! Other popular boy's names were Basil, Chauncey, Hobart, and Romeo!

Chapter Six

WACKY INVENTIONS FOR KIDS AND BY KIDS

A five-year-old girl invented an umbrella with a flashlight attachment! The flashlight would shine on the sidewalk so that whoever carried this umbrella on rainy nights could keep from stepping in mud puddles!

Out of stock! The Spanking Paddle was designed to make sure that parents wouldn't spank their kids too hard! The handle of the paddle was specially made to break if someone hit too hard with it! This invention is no longer on the market!

The brothers of invention! Nine-year-old Lewis Barton and his thirteen-year-old brother, Curtis Lawson, invented a special spill-proof meal tray for the family car. It kept fast food from falling on the seats, so the boys had fewer stains to clean up! In 1982 these two boys won the National Inventors Award.

Double your pleasure! The Chewing Gum Locket was invented for kids who like to chew their gum a second time—or even a third time. Kids could wear the locket on a chain around their neck. Inside the locket was a compartment to hold their <u>used</u> chewing gum until they were ready to chew it again!

A teenage ice cream vendor invented the ice cream cone at the St. Louis World's Fair in 1904! Arnold Fornachou ran out of ice cream dishes one day, so he bought some soft wafers from the pastry booth next to his ice cream stand. He rolled the wafers into cones and filled them with ice cream. His customers loved this new taste treat and called it the "World's Fair cornucopia"!

In 1933 three Ohio boys racing homemade wooden cars gave a newspaper photographer the idea for a new kind of race. He called it the Soap Box Derby because some of the cars were made from soap crates. Today kids still race homemade cars every year in the Soap Box Derby.

A little girl's messy drinking from a straw gave her father the idea for a very useful invention—the bendable straw! Now when kids sitting at a table are too short to reach to the top of a regular straw, they can use a flexible plastic straw to prevent sloppy spills!

A third-grade boy came up with the idea for a water-sprinkling comb—perfect for slicking down unruly hair in the morning!

Have you ever heard of the Forget-Me-Not zipper alarm? Little boys are reminded to "zip up" with this handy device. It attaches to the pants zipper and rings if the fly comes open!

Chapter Seven

BE MY BABY!

Let it snow! No baby had ever been born in Antarctica until 1978, when Emilio Palma was delivered! That's because no one lived there until the 1940s, when explorers and scientists began to set up bases on the vast frozen continent.

Pink or blue? When they first start growing inside their mothers, girl and boy babies look just the same! Only after a baby has been growing inside the mother for about six weeks does the "embryo" begin to look like a boy or a girl!

An eight-month-old baby in California passed the Red Cross water safety beginner's test! Frederick Garcia couldn't walk yet, but he could swim!

More than 30,000 sets of twins are born in the U.S. each year! Twins of all ages from around the world can meet other twins at the annual gathering of the International Twins Association. Prizes are awarded for the twins that look most alike and most different from each other.

Say "Cheese"! Babies today can have their pictures taken before they're born! Sonograms are "sound pictures" that doctors take with special ultrasonic equipment. Sound waves pass though the mother's body and produce a picture of the baby on a screen. This can sometimes show the parents whether a baby is a boy or a girl!

A newborn baby's heart beats twice as fast as a grown-up's—120 beats per minute, and a baby also breathes twice as fast, about 33 times a minute!

The average baby has his or her diaper changed about 3,000 times a year!

Babies have more bones than grown-ups! A newborn baby has more than 300 bones in his or her body, but a grown-up has only 206. This is because some of the bones (the bones in the skull, for instance) grow together to make bigger bones as the body grows.

Newborn babies don't have tears when they cry! This is because the lachrymal glands (the part of the body that makes tears) are still not developed.

Boy, do you need a wrinkle cream! Newborn babies have baggy, wrinkled skin because their skin is really too big for them! A baby grows <u>into</u> his or her skin after about six months!

All babies are born with blue eyes! At least their eyes <u>look</u> blue because of the way light reflects off of them. Actually, a baby's eyes aren't any color. It takes several weeks before their body can produce enough pigment to make the eyes black, brown, green, or truly baby blue!

Babies are usually about five months old when their first tooth comes in. But in 1638 the queen of France had a baby that was born with two teeth!

Babies dream more than older people! And it's not just because they sleep more. Babies dream during half their time asleep, but adults dream during only a quarter of their sleep time.

Chapter Eight

ARE YOU KID-DING?

The Barbie doll was named after a real little girl, Barbie Handler! Her parents noticed that she liked paper dolls that were teenagers instead of babies. They thought a teenage doll might be appealing to lots of little girls, so, in 1959, they made the first Barbie doll in their garage.

Do you know what a googol is? It's a one followed by a hundred zeros! Nine-year-old Milton Sirotta, nephew of a mathematician, came up with this name. Today scientists accept it as the proper term for this number!

Cut the deck! Three brothers in Pennsylvania built a six-story card house out of all kinds of cards—baseball cards, game cards, and regular playing cards. They used a total of 2,200 cards to build the house, and it took them five hours.

The sign reads: "NO BREATHING PLEASE"

Talk about being in a hurry! When he was two years old, William James Sidis could type in English and in French! He was admitted to Harvard University when he was only eleven!

In 1977 eight-year-old Richard Knecht did sit-ups for eleven hours! He set a record at the time for doing more than 25,000 sit-ups, which made him the world sit-up champion and one of the youngest world-record holders ever!

Coast to coast! Eleven-year-old Thomas Gregory swam all the way from France to England! He set a world record for being the youngest person to swim across the English Channel. He swam the 21 miles in only twelve hours!

No horsing around! In 1911 two boys, ages nine and twelve, rode horses across the United States— from New York City to San Francisco! Their trip took two months.

Boing! Boing! Boing! In 1974 a thirteen-year-old California girl jumped on her pogo stick for more than five hours straight! Tina Smilkstein jumped 36,218 times without falling off!

Three kids in New Hampshire slept outside every night for eight years! Rain, ice, snow, and below-zero temperatures couldn't keep Kari, Sven, and Per Heistad from going to bed in sleeping bags on their front porch. After their dad had slept on the porch for six months, the kids (who were eight, five, and three years old) decided they could beat their dad's record—and did they ever!

Bag it! Two girls in Maryland decided to see who could carry their lunch in the <u>same</u> brown paper bag for the longest time. The winner used the <u>same</u> lunch bag for 144 days!

1 2 3 4 5 6 7 8 9 10 11 12 13
14 15 16 17 18 19 20 21 22 23 24 25
26 27 28 29 30 31 32 33 34 35 36 37
38 39 40 41 42 43 44 45 46 47 48 49
50 51 52 53 54 55 56 57 58 59 60 61
62 63 64 65 66 67 68 69 70 71 72 73 74 75
76 77 78 79 80 81 82 83 84 85 86 87 88 89
90 91 92 93 94 95 96 97 98 99 100 101
102 103 104 105 106 107 108 109 110
111 112 113 116 117 118 119
120 121 122 125 126 127 128
129 130 131 135 136 137 138
139 140 144 145

Marathon boy! In 1977 an eight-year-old boy ran the New York City Marathon! Wesley Paul ran 26 miles in three hours, setting a world record for his age group!

The eleventh hour! An eleven-year-old boy in Canada was stuck in an elevator for eleven hours! The boy's only comment was that he was very happy he wasn't any older!

Leap, frog! Every year kids travel to Louisiana to enter their pet frogs in the International Frog Derby. This frog-jumping contest awards first prize to the frog that can jump the farthest.

Every year kids in Michigan run a relay race in their underwear! The race takes place in Cedar Springs, a town well known for the red flannel underwear made there. During the race, contestants put on a pair of red flannels, run a short distance, then take off the flannels and pass them on to the next team member!

Please spell "psoriasis"! More than 8 million kids compete in spelling bees every year! The National Spelling Bee is held in Washington D.C., with a first prize of $1,000. Please spell "croissant"!

Chapter Nine

BUSINESS IS BUSINESS

That's write! A four-year-old girl from Washington, D.C., wrote a book and sold it to a publisher! Dorothy Straight's book, <u>How the World Began</u>, was published two years later in 1962, when she was six.

For thirty-five cents a day, neighbors left their pets with thirteen-year-old Patti Hokr while away on vacation. Little did they know that their pets would have a vacation, too! Patti provided her animal guests with supervised play, exercise, and room service twice a day!

All aboard! Seven hundred children, ages ten to fourteen, run a real railroad line in Budapest, Hungary! The Pioneer Railway services a 7-mile track to a ski resort, a campground, and a theater.

Kristie Redding of Montana has been finding dinosaur fossils in her backyard since she was six years old! When Kristie excavated one dinosaur bone that was 4 feet long, she donated it to a local museum!

Chapter Ten

KIDS 'R US

Children without brothers and sisters used to be unusual, but not anymore! Today there are about 50 percent more only children in the U.S. than there were twenty years ago. The cost of raising children has grown over the years so more parents are choosing to have only one child.

What do they want to know? Don't ask! Specialists estimate that the average four-year-old asks more than 400 questions every day! That's about thirty questions every waking hour.

Some kids' toys today were originally tools used by hunters, soldiers, and priests! Philippine hunters threw enormous Yo-Yos that tripped and caught wild animals. In China, colorful kites were flown in special patterns to send signals between army camps. And tribal priests in many different cultures first used rattles to scare away evil spirits!

One out of every ten kids is left-handed! Many years ago, eating and writing with the left hand was thought to be abnormal. But now parents and teachers encourage kids to use the hand they feel more comfortable using.

Throughout the world, boys and girls are about 6 inches taller than kids who lived more than 100 years ago. Girls generally stop growing by the time they're sixteen years old. Boys grow until they're about eighteen.

Identical twin girls in California invented a language that only they could understand. Grace and Virginia Kennedy understood each other so well that they could talk to each other through a language of mispronounced and made-up words!

Kids wear out their socks and underwear in about one year, coats and bathing suits in two years. A baseball glove has a life of about ten years!

The last word in toys today is the videogame! American kids spend billions of dollars each year on this high-tech toy. And to think that electronic games are based on a system first developed in the 1960s for use in spacecraft.